EVERGREEN

EVERGREEN

DECORATING WITH COLOURS OF THE SEASON

Collaborators Publishing
Atlanta, Georgia

By

JILL HELMER   JOHN GRADY BURNS   KATHY STEWART

Photography by
Bartram Nason

EVERGREEN

For information contact John Grady Burns, 1440 Monroe Dr., Atlanta, GA 30324 or visit http://www.evergreencoloursoftheseason.com

Published by Collaborators Publishing

The design, printing, and marketing of *Evergreen – Colours of the Season* were coordinated by Bookhouse Group, Inc., Atlanta, Georgia. Bookhouse can be found at www.Bookhouse.net or 404.885.9515.

Edited by Jill Helmer

Designed by Laurie Porter of Compóz Design, LLC, laurie@compoz.com or 904.261.8501

Photographs by Bartram Nason, except:
pp. 33 by Bill Linsenby
pp. 108 by Jill Helmer
pp. 114 by Bill Lisenby (fireplace)

ISBN 978-0-615-30210-2

TO OUR MOTHERS, ANNE AND THERESÉ

"You know it will be a perfect Christmas – the angels will see to that."

—ANONYMOUS

ACKNOWLEDGMENTS

Creating Evergreen has been a project of love and hard work for several years. This dream could not have been realized without the countless hours of dedication from our photographer, Bartram Nason. It was a learning experience for the four of us in our artistic abilities, in patience and in perseverance.

Thank you does not seem to be enough to Angela Askew who was indispensable at so many shoots. Her contacts and ability to find just the right prop, to kick in with new ideas, to show up with meals when we were losing steam, to help us pack and unpack, to haul trees and wreaths with us, and most of all, her unwavering enthusiasm kept us going. Angela, there's not another like you. Rebecca Hudson, a dear friend and one of the most creative designers, was on call when we needed her expertise. On those occasions when one of us was unavailable, she would willingly fill in and bring a fresh approach and perspective to each shoot with an attention to detail and a knowledge of etiquette accuracy. Rebecca, thank you for sharing your extraordinary talent, for believing in us, and for working on what always seemed like the coldest days of the year.

A friend of a friend, thank you Rob Levin for the professional guidance and support you gave to this project from the first day. Without your enthusiasm and belief in us, and without your counsel, this project would never have gotten off the ground. Thank you and the Bookhouse Group for taking us on and continuing to steer us throughout this project.

Laurie Porter, our art director, thank you for being able to read our minds and know exactly what we wanted. Your ability to sort through the photographs and turn the images into a book has been one of the most life changing experiences for us.

We are indebted to our wonderful friends and clients who allowed us into their homes, and to those who loaned us their personal treasures and time:

Roe Pitts, Michele and Charlie Mitchell, Cary and Charles Calhoun, Bob Dimm, Debbie and Grover Pagano, David Jenkins and John Smith, Ford LeBoutillier, Harriet Adams and Jeff Harvey, Bonnie and Frank Creighton, Elaine and Jerry Luxemburger, Mary, Eric, Mae, and Harper Busco, Diane and Frank Lankford, Kara and David Fentress, Medra Ashmore and Maxine Hicks, Conway and John Hubbard, Bethany Vaughn, Pam McCoy, Anne Fuzey, Jane and Bob Long, John Lunsford, Linda and Buster Jenkins, Annette and Charles Burns, Melanie Kennedy, Conner Burns, Paul Burns, Kitty Bray, Betty and David Paradise, Joe and Cindy Meng, Gina Latham, Jerold and Betty Krouse, Studie and Zach Young, Suzanne Dansby Bollman, Elizabeth Kane, Anneliese Vogt-Harber, Lucy and Bill Vance, Karen and Stephen Klare, Dan Cleveland and Jeffrey Rogerson. We are equally grateful to Bob Amick and the staff at Parish Restaurant, Dan Belman and Randy Korando and the staff of Boxwoods Gardens & Gifts, the Historic Natchez City Cemetery, the staff at Vogt Riding Academy, and the staff of the Georgia Governor's Mansion, for allowing us to shoot on their premises.

To add just a bit more pizzazz to our shoots, we would like to thank the following for providing us with beautiful accessories to work with:

- *BBj Linen – Atlanta, Georgia*
- *J. Brown for the Home – Texarkana, Texas*
- *As You Like It Silver Shop, Different Accents, D. Short Furniture, Cornerstone Antiques, Edna's Cake Creations – Natchez, Mississippi*
- *And of course, to our families and our partners in life, Ned, John, and Michael, who continued to encourage us and let us hold steadfast to our dream.*

Thank you
to those
who helped

CONTENTS

"*Twas the night before Christmas . . .*"

INTRODUCTION

Evergreen is about two things – your home, and how to breathe the spirit of Christmas into it. The idea for this book was conceived by us during the Christmas holidays. Over a glass of wine, the three of us were celebrating the completion of a decorating job well done. Sitting by a crackling fire and amongst some of our own designs, we began comparing our individual traditions and those of our families. We realized our ideas and traditions were something we wanted to share with others; the book idea was born. Over the next several years we photographed and chronicled the various holiday decorating jobs we did for our clients, our friends, as well as many of the decorations in our personal homes.

There may be some photographs here that inspire your own creativity to soar; while others may show you something you can imitate with the least amount of effort. Surrounded by your own treasures, you will find it sometimes takes very little to transform a room for the holidays. It can be as simple as changing the candles to red, bringing in a cluster of nandina berries to put in that otherwise empty container, or just displaying your favorite childhood ornament twirled with a beautiful satin ribbon.

Today, there is a generation that lived through the Great Depression. For many of them, their fondest Christmas memories are from their childhoods. They had very little monetarily, but that failed to thwart their anticipation and excitement for the holiday. Their merriment was generated from the games they played, from sitting spellbound in front of the tree looking at the tinsel's reflections of their few cherished ornaments, and from baking sweets and strudels that today we would only think of purchasing.

The next generation, too, has some wonderful memories from their childhoods. Who doesn't remember waiting for the power company to string the Christmas lights across Main Street, the anticipation of waiting for the stores to complete their window dressings, or the whole family piling into the car to go pick out the tree, or hoping that the key to the shiny metal skates in the department store window would soon be hanging around your neck? Perhaps you flocked your tree with Ivory snow flakes, made tree ornaments of styrofoam balls covered with sequins, pearl-headed pins and ribbons, or spent hours preparing for the church's Christmas program. Whatever your memories, these are the stories we might have forgotten to share while helping the current generation prepare for their holiday. Perhaps it's time to dust off these left-over memories and share a bit of nostalgia with those you hold dear to you.

The holidays should be a time to be enjoyed. We have allowed shopping, pageants, parties and other occasions to fill our time and become substitutes for Christmas. Before these events became popular, we drew upon our memories of Christmas traditions to provide the entertainment for our families and friends. We hope this book will inspire you to stay at home and revive old traditions or make new ones in the warmth of your home. Bringing Christmas into your home should be a happy experience that memories can be built upon. If you make it such, you will be more inclined to have friends in, and you will find that you and your family will enjoy not only the holidays more, but also being with each other. It will give you the opportunity to share your stories and memories, whether it be the metal skates you received or the times shared with your family. You just might discover the true spirit of Christmas. I know the three of us have.

We hope you find *Evergreen* to be a treasure that brings you not only ideas, but peace and joy as you turn each page.

—*Jill Helmer, John Grady Burns, Kathy Stewart*

GET READY, GET SET, GO

It seems the leftovers from Thanksgiving dinner are barely put away when the conversation turns to Christmas. Suddenly, it's the weekend of Thanksgiving and you find yourself dragging the Christmas decorations down from the attic or up from the basement. Is it really all necessary?

The next several weeks should be one of the most beautiful and festive times of the year. Christmas decorating should not be exhausting or overwhelming; if it is, then you are making it so. If putting up a tree is tiring and too time consuming for you, then don't do it. There are countless ways to bring the festive spirit into your home without the labor intensive job of putting up a tree, lighting it, and decorating it; and let us not forget, taking it all down in a couple of weeks.

On the other hand, if putting up a tree is your favorite part of the holiday, then by all means make it the priority on your decorating list and cut back on some of the other duties you have assigned yourself.

If shopping for a cast of thousands is overwhelming, then figure out a way to simplify your gift giving. If shopping is your favorite part, then do not forget to stop at the nursery and pick up a couple of branches of ilex and freshly cut evergreens to make your home festive and fragrant. This may be all it takes to add a touch of Christmas to some of your rooms.

Whatever you do for the holidays, take more time to enjoy yourself, your family, and the warmth of your home. The Christmas season is one of the most beguiling times of year. Winter provides us with ample opportunity to burn those candles just a little bit longer and to curl up in the comfort of our beautifully decorated homes.

A Traditional Christmas
Ornaments collected over the years decorate this beautifully shaped Fraser fir tree. The family's train set is put out every year and continues to delight guests of all ages.

THE SPIRIT OF CHRISTMAS

To some, Christmas would not be complete without the tree. To others, the tree is secondary or even nonexistent in their decorating. Bringing fir, cedar, pine, holly, and mistletoe into the house provides not only a visual delight, but invigorates us with a fragrance of nature during what is often a gray and bleak time of year. The spirit of Christmas can be gained by looking around and seeing the dazzling red berries on the different varieties of hollies, the crimson red of a shrub's leaves that turned red in late fall and has retained its color for winter, and the bright red cardinals resting on bare branches of the trees.

It is a reminder that Mother Nature provides us with beauty year round. People who love Christmas love it because of the way it makes them feel. Christmas is coming; retailers have advertisied for many weeks, but that does not mean we will catch the spirit we are seeking. For many, the spirit of Christmas is knowing that family or friends from out of town will be arriving, children will be home from school, the tradition of Christmas dinner, the excitement of Christmas morning with little ones, or perhaps it is just the peacefulness found at home—the reasons are as diverse as they are plenty.

We have a nostalgia associated with Christmas that goes back to our childhoods and the many wonderful times we shared with family and friends. Somewhere in the past, a deposit of memories was made that has continued to grow with interest and has deepened the sentimentality in our minds over the years. Perhaps this is the cornerstone for the perfect Christmas that so many seek. The spirit of Christmas can not be found wrapped in a package under the tree, or stuffed into a stocking; nor is it available in a jar from the grocer. The Christmas spirit is in our hearts.

Partying in Holiday Style
The untraditional colors of chartreuse and turquoise take on a festive and more formal holiday feel when combined with the gold glittered reindeer.

> **❝** *Lanterns lining the path for guests, cast a blue reflection on the cold wet pavement.* **❞**

Outdoor Living with Holiday Flair

A variety of evergreens not only dresses up this mailbox, but adds warmth to the harshness of the stone wall behind it.

Providing color to the winter garden also becomes a source of food for our feathered friends.

The addition of nandina berries on a grapevine wreath is the perfect complement to the simplicity of this garden's entrance.

Hedgeapples and sugar cones fill in this container's void where summer and fall flowers have no longer survived. As January and harsher months approach, more cones can be added as plant material slowly diminishes.

Red lights, red berries, and a few select red vintage ornaments produce a warm and cozy ambiance to this library. With an all-red tree, very little, if any, additional Christmas decor is required for the room.

" *Nothing says Christmas like the color red and nothing says red like ilex branches.* **"**

Tall branches of winged elm mixed with ilex berries take these arrangements to the ceiling, making them appear even more dramatic when combined with the simple branches of pine and sugar cones on the mantel shelf.

inspirational interiors   Roger Banks-Pye

(opposite page)
Pheasants tucked into a honeysuckle-entwined tree lend just the right touch of wildlife to this informally decorated fir. The natural decor was chosen to complement the antelope-patterned carpet used on the stairs.

(top left)
A hedge of Leyland cypress serves as the perfect Christmas backdrop for a lone winterberry holly.

(top right)
Pheasants seem at home here as the focal point in a brass galley tray used in this tablescape with cedar, pine, magnolia, boxwood, and pine cones.

(bottom left)
Magnolia garland studded with ilex berries warms this putto standing guard at the fireplace surround.

Dressed in Winter White

The winter wonderland display in this retail shop affords the opportunity to bring in shimmering and frosted shades of silver, gold, platinum, and glass accessories. A little touch of silver and gold can be great accents, but when combined with a base color of platinum, as in these trees, they become softer and can be used in excess without appearing as heavy or as overdone as silver and gold can sometimes be.

◀ Heavy Spanish moss draping the exterior live oak trees dictates a lush magnolia wreath as the obvious choice for the doors of this plantation in the Deep South.

▲ Spanish moss hanging from the lichen-covered branches was clipped from the grounds of the plantation and incorporated into a massive arrangement of berries and cedar also collected from the property.

Stables in Style

All work places, in this case, a riding academy, can reflect the festive season of the holidays. The gate to the property is decorated with a mixed fir and cedar wreath decorated with holly, cones, and tangerines. The barn doors hold metal wire baskets filled with tangerines and topped with arrangements of ilex, pyracantha, and holly.

A Stable of Beauty

"Whence comes this rush of wings afar, Following straight the Noel star? Birds from the woods in wondrous flight, Bethlehem seek this Holy Night."

—CAROL OF THE BIRDS

Sitting atop the mailbox, this Cape Cod-style birdhouse is the home to a family of wrens.

A replica of a Tennessee country schoolhouse, this bird house has been home to a family of wrens for many years.

This North Carolina birdhouse, made by a local woodworker, was purchased and painted for Christmas one year as a family art project.

Tucked into the top of the
tree, this nest is seen when
descending the nearby
staircase. Berries, cones,
and birds are the only other
decor on the tree.

33

$\mathcal{A}$ Feast to Remember

This fourth-generation dining table was originally designed to seat sixteen people.
The family grew so much over the years that the table was transformed into a large
buffet table during the holidays.

COLOUR

While some feel that red and green are the only colors to decorate with during the holidays, there are those that take it up a notch by using rich golds and sparkling silvers. Consider shaking up your traditional decor and use the opulent colors of jewel tones—those rich shades typically found in the gemstones amethyst, sapphire, emerald, ruby, and topaz. These warm colors, when used with equal depth, harmonize beautifully with each other, making distinctive combinations. A touch of any of these tones or just the use of one color can make a whole room come alive without having to saturate the room to look like a royal palace. While somewhat faded, the vintage mercury ornaments produced in the first half of the twentieth century can be a good starting point to work with. Pull them from the attic, dust off the box, and try piling them into a beautiful silver or crystal bowl. With very little effort, a new palette may be introduced into your room giving you the confidence to brighten it up even more with each year to come.

(opposite page)
Jewel-toned ornaments and tree toppers with small artificial trees and berries, combined with the long lasting fresh plant material of kalanchoes and variegated ivy, make for a whimsical planted composition in this red galvanized tub.

(above)
Not your traditional holiday color, yet this rose-colored bannister lends itself well to the bright chartreuse and red accents used in the magnolia garland.

(left)
Even the topaz-colored canaries have gotten in on the act with their jewel-toned ruby colored wreath.

❝ *Color tones used in equal depth harmonize beautifully.***❞**

The Splendor of Colour

◀ The ilex berries and fresh cut greens outside this potting shed will soon be arranged and taken indoors to their new home.

▼ These miniature cyclamen plants can withstand cold temperatures, making them ideal for use on this porch.

*O*utdoor Pleasures

Already dressed in red, these bar lamps required only a loop of ribbon to ready them for the holidays. The amber-colored lights on the front wreaths have an equally vibrant effect, aiding in creating a rich and inviting atmosphere.

Ruby-colored Murano glass chandeliers from the mid 1900's shine brilliantly against the old bricks in this restaurant's stairwell.

43

It's in the Details

A small Eastern red cedar tree with winterberry branches amassed from the countryside make a beautiful arrangement for the table in this mountain retreat. The smallest of details from the Araucana egg nestled in the tiniest of bird nests, the hedgeapples from the Osage orange tree, and the hare seeking warmth under his red ribbon muffler are all details that make this woodland vignette a warm and cozy spot.

This unique bark top coat is actually designed to hold a bottle of wine. It has been pressed into service as an additional accessory in this charming tablescape.

Venetian wine glasses, commissioned by the owner on a trip to Italy, are a graceful and elegant addition to this beautifully set table.

Lasting Impressions

This beautiful entrance to the Natchez City Cemetery, c. 1822,
is home to some of the most beautiful ironwork in the country.
Almost all patterns and styles of iron craftsmanship produced
in the nineteenth and early twentieth centuries in America is
represented throughout this Mississippi cemetery.

A close up from the gate of the weeping angel (opposite page) shows the intricate details on a basket of fruit and flowers.

As long as this massive live oak stands, so will the stone column so lavishly decorated to greet visitors during the holidays. Even the mockingbird atop the post wants to get into the spirit.

Large sugar cones with cedar and fir
garland swags decorate the entrance to the
iron tasseled gate of a family plot.

Pyracantha berries are used to dress
up the elaborate iron work around the
weeping angel.

" *Trees can be put anywhere and in any room—from a home office to a dining room.* **"**

Deck the Halls

Stockings hung other than on the mantel provide an opportunity to change your decorating styles from year to year.

O Tannenbaum takes on a contemporary look with this ficus tree surrounded by a pavé of red carnations. This decorated ficus is the perfect solution for a small space that renders no room to bring in a fir tree for the season.

55

" *Entertaining like royalty is all in the presentation.* **"**

The simple setting for this dessert buffet appears much more formal and elaborate due to the beautiful shades and textures of golds and reds that predominate.

Simple Elegance

(opposite page)
So as not to compete with the the rich colors of the walls
and the painting, unadorned wreaths are chosen for the
front entrance to this home.

(above)
The simplicity of a couple branches of ilex and a bare
branch adds drama to this end table. An old imari bowl
filled with green bulbs and a nosegay of roses and fir is
all that is needed to complete this setting.

❝ *The simplest of decorations can make the
most elaborate statement.* **❞**

Awaiting Santa

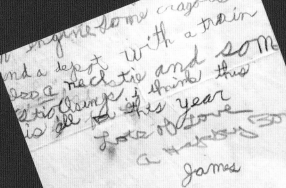

A Letter to Santa
This 1924 keepsake letter to Santa requesting "a depot with a train, along with a necktie," is a reminder that Christmas wishes have changed very little over the years, except maybe for the tie.

ENTERTAINING

Entertaining today has never been easier, yet so few people receive guests into their own homes. There are so many markets carrying prepared food items, wines, desserts, and even flowers, that planning and executing an event is not as daunting as it once was. Most of us have beautiful china, silver, and crystal, keeping it stored away and saved for that special occasion. That occasion is here—the holidays. This is a season that calls for using your finest items even if the event does not necessarily require using them. These niceties are what will help make memories for you, your friends, and your family. People love the comfort and indulgence of being entertained in the coziness of a home and they love seeing and using fine flatware and crystal. The house is decorated, now show it off. Whether it be a small intimate dinner party or the large dinner buffet seen here, the only leftovers at the end of the occasion will be memories.

(above)
The gorgeous all-white arrangement becomes the focal point against the dark red walls and rich bronze colored cloth. Flowers intertwined in the iron chandelier give the llusion of a candelabrum in the arrangement.

(left)
China with the hostess's initials painted by William Lycett of Atlanta, Georgia, was a popular custom amongst the well-to-do in late nineteenth century.

This small cedar serves as the couple's Christmas tree. The arduous job of putting up a large tree was replaced with the table-top size which allowed for more elaborate decorations in the room.

Table Top Trees

Today convenience, lifestyle, and decor may dictate the practicality or reason to have a small table top tree, but to the eighteenth-century English, it was a tradition from the influence of their German neighbors. Each member of the family would have a small tree on a separate table with their personal gifts stacked under it. While this may seem excessive today, having just one table top tree can make a big statement in a small space. A small tree stand is ideal for putting directly into the container or urn to be used; otherwise, the tree can be placed directly into a large piece of tightly wedged floral foam.

> " *A table-top tree can be the perfect solution when a large tree is not an option.* "

Setting the Mood

Nothing sets a mood like the glow of candlelight. While social etiquette may frown upon candles used before dusk, gray winter days can be an exception, especially for a holiday celebration.

This 1920's cottage is decorated simply, yet still has several strong focal points.

❝ *Window boxes are not only great architectural features, but they provide another element of the house that can easily be decorated for the season.* **❞**

Standing Guard
Hutch and Oliver, wearing their festive
Christmas collars, patiently wait for the
arrival of the first guests.

Nourishing the Senses

THE GARDEN

Nothing gets one more in the mood for Christmas than shopping for the tree, wreaths, garlands, plants, and holiday accessories. The fragrance gleaned from just walking into a nursery or a farmer's market nourishes the senses and compels one to take a time out for Christmas. It is here in the nursery that restraint tends to be thrown out the window. There is such a variety of items that can be purchased today that up until a decade ago were only enjoyed from books and magazines. Magnolia garlands and wreaths, once only prevalent in the South, are shipped everywhere as well as Port Orford cedars and Douglas firs that are shipped nationwide from the West. Not only do these products beckon us to take them home, but ideas for decorating our gardens as well as our homes become abundant. Most homes afford a view of the yard that is seen from an area in the house where a lot of time is spent. Decorating the garden should be as natural as decorating the interior of the home. Afterall, it is a view seen everyday and should bring as much joy to you as the decked halls within your home. A garland wrapped around the birdhouse pole, a wreath on the garage window or back gate, a tree with popcorn and apples for the birds are all simple touches that can bring unmeasurable amounts of pleasure.

Finding a Home
Planted compositions wait to go home
from this retail shop.

Apothecary jars filled with fruit make a strong decorative statement with very little decorating talent required. If wishing to use for long term, artificial fruit would be more practical.

> *Your personal treasures can take on a Christmas look by adding a few winter berries or simply displaying a favorite ornament.*

A branch of pomegranates, along with nandina berries stuck directly into the philodendron's soil, will hold their color for several weeks.

With the shift of a few accessories, this acorn tree fits into place as if it were made for the table.

For the holiday season, St. Nick replaces the traditional bookend.

The Stable Party

"Jingle Bells" has long been a song associated with the holidays since its origination in 1822. It immediately conjures up images of sleigh rides in the snow, bells, hot chocolate, and woolen blankets. It is from these sights and sounds that we pull together ideas for our own gatherings. Once the frost has melted away, there is nothing more enjoyable than gathering with friends to prepare for a ride. Bells on the wreaths, a woolen blanket used in place of a tablecloth, and an assortment of biscuits and pastries await the group before riding out.

Horsing Around

A pair of massive wreaths hung on both sides of the stable doors are there to greet one and all as well as the horses and stable hands working on the inside.

For intimate gatherings, a desk is ideal set up as
the bar. A slender table-top cedar tree makes
the area even cozier with the high ceilings.
An arrangement of nandina berries balances
the red candles.

A collection of glass swizzle sticks, crystal
glasses, and glass grapes all sparkle from
the glow of the candles' flames.

$\mathcal{W}$arm Welcomes

Style at the Doorstep

The exterior decorations of a home, usually set the tone for the interior decorations. The simplicity of an evergreen wreath or a cluster of pine cones adorned with only a simple red bow can create a coziness and warmth that immediately summons one in. If there are additional exterior decorations, they need to complement the décor used on the door.

> **"** When sharing the street with others, use restraint while decorating the exterior. **"**

The clean lines and blocks of colors on the table's composition coordinate with the subtle color blocks in the Chinese screen.

At home in a basket of boxwood and fir, this large mercury glass acorn makes quite a statement.

The homeowner's fondness for acorns shows up again on the top of this antique tureen lid.

Party-Ready

A sampling from an extensive collection of colored glass votives, bowls, and stemware is used during the holidays as candle holders.

A large silver tureen filled with shiny and matte glass bulbs works beautifully with the texture of the red damask linen.

In this room full of rich colors and so many textures,
an undecorated fir wreath hung only with red silk
ribbon is all that is needed.

THE CHRISTMAS TREE

Today you can walk into most any department store or garden center and be surprised at the way a tree has been trimmed. These same feelings were probably similar as far back as the twelfth century when European Christians were hanging fir trees upside down from their ceilings as a symbol of Christianity. There are just as many legends tracing the first tree and the use of evergreens as a symbol for Christmas, as there are trying to identify the accurate story and associating it with a specific country. The legend that remains the most popular is that of Martin Luther during the winter of 1500. While out walking he was so overcome by the beauty of the snow-covered trees shimmering in the moonlight, that he took a small fir tree home for his family. He decorated it with candles to mimic the glistening light of the beautiful site he'd witnessed; this is considered the first lighted tree.

History tells us it was probably the Hessian troops that brought their tradition of the fir tree to America during the American Revolution. As a Protestant tradition, the custom of having this small table-top tree decorated with apples, nuts, and paper was slow to grow. Meanwhile, the popularity of the tree was growing in Germany and Austria. Queen Victoria's marriage to Prince Albert of Germany helped to advance the popularity of the tree throughout Great Britain and Europe in the early 1800's. Eager to embrace

the practices of the British royalty, the public was quick to imitate their same traditions. Slow to catch on, the Americans did not embrace the idea of a large tree until the mid nineteenth century.

(above)
Strobus cones from the Eastern white pine tree are the perfect shape for cascading over the lip of a container.

(top left)
The orange drapes create a blank canvas for the ilex berries and winged elm in this all-natural arrangement.

Santa ornaments collected throughout the years make this tree unique.

O Christmas Tree

Hydrangeas harvested in the fall were used to make an unorthodox tree in a traditional home.

A Chinese cloisonné and brass bowl that otherwise sits empty, is the ideal container for this small fir.

Tiny candles that mimic Christmas bulb ornaments are a departure from the traditional candles normally used.

A pair of porcelain Boston Terriers stands guard before a bowl of lady apples.

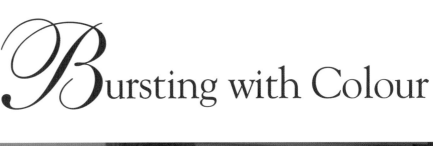

Bursting with Colour

Floral Décor

Entertaining on a grand scale provides the perfect opportunity to pull out all the stops. Nothing is more elegant than a home decorated with fresh flowers during the Christmas season, in this case an 1830's plantation outside Natchez, Mississippi. *(left)* The large basket arrangement hangs on a nine-foot interior hall door that had previously been the home's front door. The family pet, Buster, poses for his Christmas photo. *(above)* Amaryllis and parrot tulips incorporated into a sizable arrangement of holly, winterberry, cedar, and dusty miller make a striking statement in this large living room.

The mixture of textures and dark rich colors adds to the warmth and coziness of the winter meal to be served.

IT'S TIME TO CELEBRATE!

The exterior decorations of a home usually reflect what the interior holds. The twinkling of lights from the tree in the window, the wreaths and garland adorning the windows or door are inviting to all those who have come calling. Before even passing through the foyer, guests have a desire to settle in for the occasion at hand —be it dropping in for a holiday hello, a hot cup of tea, a warm toddy, or an evening meal shared with friends. The simplicity of the decorations, whether it be a table-top tree, a glorious towering twelve-foot fir, or a porcelain full of holly and ilex berries brings comfort to us.

Decorations that we associate as traditional, or the expected, provide us with a sense of serenity. There are those who prefer a more unrestrained style for their interior decorations. For these homes, one enters knowing tradition and calm will not be there to receive them. Instead, they will be greeted by an element of surprise with the interior decorations. This departure from traditional design can even produce a visual overload for the senses. Overwhelmed with trying to take it all in, the excitement from the stimulation the eye and the soul experience can only be paralleled to the frenzy of the holidays. Forget the background music of Tchaikovsky's "The Nutcracker;" bring on "Deck the Halls" by Manheim Steamroller. It's time to celebrate!

Whether the exterior and interior decorations both send the same message is an individual decision. We all like to express our individuality, but it is best done indoors and not outdoors as a street competition. Indoors, our individual personalities should shine for ourselves, our families, and our friends. The holidays are a personal experience for each individual with the decorations reflecting who you are. Whatever your décor, friends will leave your home with a gift of Christmas spirit.

Awaiting Arrival

Collecting vintage tree ornaments today has become a pastime for many. The mercury glass ornaments produced in Eastern Europe and the United States in the first half of the twentieth century are getting more difficult to find. The nostalgia associated with these ornaments brings memories and traditions of the holidays closer to our heart. Here, a collection of vintage bell ornaments fills a tree lit by the larger old-fashioned clear bulbs.

> **"** *Christmas is the perfect time to unbox and display those childhood toys from the attic.* **"**

❝Sometimes the simplicity of a bowl of pinecones, apples, or ornaments is all that is needed.**❞**

A light dusting of snow on the bare branches adds to the winter feel of the composition on this mantel.

Cardinal Rules

Winter Wonderland

A simple arrangement of Polo roses and cedar adds to the elegance and formality of this intimate dinner party.

> **The English tradition of Christmas crackers, usually pulled before or after Christmas dinner, appeals to all ages.**

The antique Chinoiserie chest holds a large arrangement of ilex, cedar, bare branches, and gold curly willow that further enhances the intimate setting of this table.

111

THE WREATH

Wreaths of different shapes have become popular today. Rectangular, oval, and square are fashionable, but to those who prefer the traditional round, it is a symbol representing the circle of life. Wreaths can be made from many materials, but those made of evergreen symbolize everlasting life, because the evergreen, never losing its leaves, even in the most bitter of cold, lives on forever.

Garland of gold silk leaves, chartreuse ornaments, and gold and green striped ribbon are intertwined throughout this lush cedar garland giving it an elegant and lively look.

A photograph tucked amongst these accessories becomes a part of this Christmas vignette.

A farmhouse mantel glows with subtle light from the votives and candles while the Moravian star atop the column adds additional soft light. Bailey sleeps in her favorite chair.

Some years the collection of porcelain and glass trees is moved to this table leaving the mantel available for a simpler look.

115

Ring in the Holidays

I heard the bells on Christmas Day
Their old, familiar carols play,
And wild and sweet
The words repeat
Of peace on earth, goodwill to men!

—HENRY WADSWORTH LONGFELLOW

The warm and soft glow in this foyer indicates a peaceful and relaxing evening is in store for the guests.

Enchanting Pleasures of the Season

This detail from a vignette shows a miniature conservatory filled with treasures.

A wreath attached to an overhead kitchen light fixture displays favorite glass ornaments.

Additional lighting on the porch serves to showcase
the oversized wreaths on the French doors as well as
light up the home for the holidays.

Covered with clematis vines in the warmer months, the lighted silhouettes of these topiary forms glow in the garden after the dusting of an early December snowfall.

Birds bundled in winter clothing are suspended from branches above a vignette of miniature trees, a conservatory, and an assortment of nests.

A miniature tree gives shelter.

Protected and warm in their aviary, these birds look out onto the patio decorated with fresh winter greens and an abundance of ilex branches.

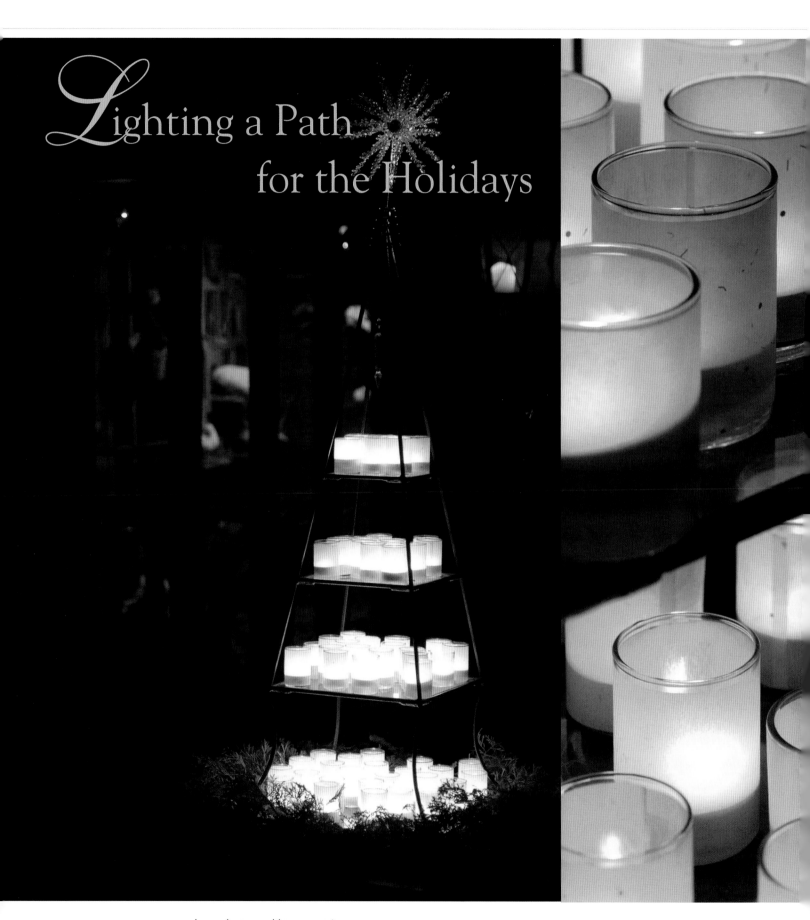

Lighting a Path for the Holidays

It may be too cold to entertain outdoors, but strategic placement of candles, lights, or luminaries viewed from a window adds additional ambiance to any event.

Votives wrapped in vellum add
a misty-like softness.

The brilliance of a Christmas star
serves to illuminate the garden.

125

66A Christmas candle is a lovely thing;
It makes no noise at all,
But softly gives itself away;
While quite unselfish, it grows small.**99**

—EVA K. LOGUE

127

Decorating with untraditional color makes this dining room come alive. With so much red already in the room, orange makes the seasonal decorations pop.

Simply Charming

An old collection of mostly
Chinese Export shows off
handsomely tucked into a
doubled cedar garland. The
early 1900's hand-hewn beam
is a deep mantel shelf that
can accommodate the garland
and staggered pillar candles
with ease.

> **"** Heap on more wood!
> The wind is chill;
> But let it whistle as it will,
> We'll keep our Christmas merry still. **"**
>
> —Sir Walter Scott

Visions of Christmas

Say red and green and visions of Christmas come to mind. Orange and red and green can be just as seasonal, but with just enough twist to make the decorations stand out with a more sophisticated look. By using the three colors together, and any of the shades in between, the designs will have more interest and blend well into your color scheme.

Inviting Entry

706

When wreaths are used on windows, a basket arrangement on the front door adds more interest and becomes the focal point of the decorations.

An old Italian putto bearing a
candelabrum lights up the night.

Symbols of the Holiday

Angels have been portrayed and used in a variety of ways during the Christmas season and have become one of the most popular and delightful symbols associated with the holiday. Greek in origin, the word angel means messenger or one who is sent. Since it was the angels that announced the arrival of Christ's birth, it has become one of the more important religious Christmas symbols.

> "*Angels we have heard on high Sweetly singing o'er the plains. . .*"

GLASS ORNAMENTS

The origination of the glass ornament is a twelfth-century invention from the German village of Lauscha. The designs were taken from their current decorations of fruits, baked cookies in various shapes, and their handmade crafts. By the mid 1800's, they had perfected using mercury to make their beautiful ornaments. By the early 1900's, other Eastern European countries began producing and exporting the ornaments to other countries, namely the United States.

With the Great Depression, and another war looming on the horizon, American businessman Max Eckhardt foresaw the interruption of imports as had happened during the first World War. He approached the Corning Company to invent a way to produce glass ornaments from their light bulb machinery—thus, the term "bulb" for what we today sometimes call Christmas balls. Successful at this endeavor, Eckhardt then established the Shiny Brite Ornaments company.

Ornaments were lacquered by machine on the outside and then decorated by hand. The following year the ornaments were silvered on the inside in order to remain "shiny bright" forever.

During World War II, material shortages forced the company to decorate the clear glass bulbs with only simple thin stripes.

Corning continued to manufacture the ornaments, but they were now experimenting with a greater number and variety of shapes and sizes. Due to World War II, many of the vintage ornaments you find today reflect the history of that period . . . the lack of silver (mercury) giving way to clear bulbs, the torpedoes used in battle giving way to the elongated "torpedo" ornaments, and the cardboard caps due to the short supply of metal.

A small 1842 Episcopal church is decorated to greet its members for Christmas Eve services.

This black tooled leather screen makes a dramatic backdrop for the arrangement of ilex branches.

143

Elegance at its Best

HOLIDAY ENTERTAINING

I t is easier to find reasons not to entertain than it is to find reasons to, yet being invited into one's home is still the ultimate invitation to receive. Friends and associates much prefer the ambiance and warmth generated in a private residence as opposed to a public place. Sometimes nostalgia plays a role in deciding what type of event to have. Opening the cabinets and finding silver and crystal pieces that your mother or grandmother once entertained with can be the impetus in choosing certain items. Once you have selected your favorites, deciding what to serve will be dictated by the pieces. Beautiful cut crystal sherry glasses would suggest a late afternoon party; dessert plates, cake stands, and coffee cups or cordials would reveal a dessert party is in your future. Choose the best you have. It is a reflection on how you feel about the guests that will be invited into your home and they in turn will be honored to have been a part of sharing your most treasured heirlooms. A reciprocal invitation could soon be waiting for you by return post.

A potted cedar available from the local nursery makes a stunning backdrop and serves to soften the brick wall behind this dessert buffet.

The sophistication of charcoal walls presents a striking backdrop for decorating during the holidays. Rich golds, bright silvers, and bold reds almost act as punctuation marks against the dark walls. Since everything pops and sometimes appears as blocks of color against the wall, less is definitely more. The single use of an item makes a statement without requiring further embellishment of accessories or excessively swagged garlands. (*top left*) The pair of red cockscomb trees worked into the garland add weight to one end of the mantel while (*top center*) the other end is kept simple with pillar candles and a single sugar cone. Other decorations in the living room are also kept to a minimum in order to make an individual and distinct statement.

"Use red and use it freely with your holiday decorating. Red will harmonize with almost every color."

Our Feathered Friends

A planter of apples and a star-shaped peanut butter treat centred in this lush boxwood wreath help keep our feathered friends fat and happy.

Surrounded by red packages, a fir decorated with all silver ornaments and heavily cloaked in tinsel takes on an almost magical appearance.

TINSEL

Many of us remember our grandparents having that magical look of shimmering icicles on their trees, or we were fortunate enough ourselves to have decorated with tinsel. Dating as far back as the early 1600's, tinsel was originally made of real silver. It was first hammered and then cut into thin strips to be used sparingly on the tree. Due to the intensive labor required, machinery was soon invented to take real silver, shred it into thin strips, and then package it for public use. However, being real silver, it easily tarnished from the smoke of the tree's candles, and also from the contact with human hands. As a result, the tinsel had to be meticulously removed from the tree, cleaned, and carefully packed away to be used again the following Christmas. It is no wonder that tinsel icicles began to lose their popularity.

By the mid 1900's, aluminum tinsel came into being and was mass produced so it could be used in excess. Today, while not widely used, tinsel is made from manufactured synthetic materials, and has a much more fluid feel and look than its ancestors of over a hundred years ago.

151

Artist's Palette

So as not to compete with or obscure the painting, the arrangement is kept low and done in the same palette as the painting.

The reflection in the mirror catches the up-close details of the arrangement beneath it and the sparkle of lights on the distant tree.

" *There is no rule that all Christmas decorations have to be red.* **"**

Blue and white always has an eye-popping effect
when teamed with shades of oranges and evergreens.
Red would have been expected and yet not nearly as
complementary to the blue.

FIRESIDE CHATS

For many, the living room is a room passed by and never used. For those of us who prefer cozy spaces over great rooms or family rooms, the living room is a place to sit and talk, relax, entertain guests, or to find solitude after a long day. No one room with a fireplace can be quite as inviting and gracious feeling than the living room, whether it be decorated formally or not. During the Christmas season, there seems to be a strong emphasis on decorating the fireplace mantel, so it should reason then that the room ought to be used and enjoyed more frequently during the holiday. Living room mantels tend to lend themselves well to more formal decorations. If stockings are to be hung, they are usually done so in the more lived-in room of the house, thus freeing up the living room mantel for a more opulent design.

Creating a Winter Wonderland

A large scale dinner party celebrating the holidays gives an opportunity to decorate more elaborately than just for personal pleasure. White is a sophisticated and neutral color to work with. It can set the mood for a room or an event, especially during the holidays when phrases and images of white as the driven snow, dancing snowflakes, and glistening icicles come to mind. Dark or strong colors can be overpowering, but when white flowers or decorations are used with them, the colors are toned down. When used with pastel colors, white can make those shades appear more prominent and help to create a soft and graceful ambiance.

The table decorations for both these events used floral arrangements atop snow-filled apothecary jars to give a hint of the winter weather outdoors. (*opposite left*) Hung on the front of mirrored doors, wreaths filled with white lilies, roses, hydrangeas, and dianthus are hung in varying sizes to mimic the shape of a Christmas tree. While both events used similar flowers, the white arrangements against the salmon-colored walls create a cozy warm feeling. (*above*) The arrangements in this light blue and gold room add a more romantic and soft ambiance.

Where Would We Be Without Red?

In a home of mostly neutral colors, a heavy use of red decorations drastically changes the feel of it. A splash of red used in each room pulls the look together, converging to a focal point in the dining room with the scarlet red table linen, ornaments, packages, and flowers.

The combination of the white roses against the vintage embroidered sheers imparts a quiet, and restful Christmas meal to come. The softness of so much white gives an ethereal feel after a season full of events, parties, and other social engagements. Pieces from a collection of copper luster are grouped together to give the appearance of one arrangement.

Packages of Every Size

The origin of gift giving can be traced to the Roman's January Festival of the Kalends. The emperor was presented gifts of evergreen branches to symbolize everlasting life and then much later, gifts of sweets, honey and cakes became more appealing. History also credits the Three Wise Men for the gifts they brought to the Christ Child as possibly starting our present day custom. It was the Victorians, however, who popularized gift giving as we know it. Gathering around the tree, gifts were bestowed to one another as an expression of love and kindness, much as it is done today.

Displays of Beauty

A collection of antique creamware is used to display a collection of vintage mercury glass tree toppers. Both collections have meticulously been cared for during the years. The tree toppers, many of them stored in their original boxes, are mostly from the Shiny Brite Company.

Roses are Red

Roses make a statement however they are used—mixed with ilex berries, japonica pieris, lenten rose, and a variety of evergreens. *(left)* Loose berries from the Burford holly fill the vase and work to hold the flowers in place.

" *Which is loveliest in a rose?*
Its coy beauty when it's budding,
or its splendour when it blows? **"**

—George Barlow

DRESS UP THE OCCASION WITH ROSES

During the holiday season, very few flowers have the presence that a red rose does. Roses have graced the dining rooms and grand halls and parlors of dignitaries, royalty, and just the plain common folk for centuries. Aside from the vibrant and intense red color, the various stages and longevity of the rose make it a flower definitely worth using in your home during the holidays. Cultivating and growing roses is a huge international industry today. Growers extolling the different varieties of their roses with different petal counts and shapes, shades, and different growing seasons, promote their product internationally to several types of vendors —flower markets and super markets, to name just two. Most of the time there is a difference in the quality that these markets receive. If you want a longer-lasting and higher-quality rose, then purchase from a reliable florist. If the goal is to have roses last only a night or two for an event, then the discounted varieties will do just fine. If roses are being purchased for a party or some form of entertaining, why not prepare ahead, purchase the roses, and enjoy them during the week prior to the party? Their true beauty is best seen somewhere between half open and full blown. A tight rose has no place at a special event.

Cottage Charm

Seen from across the garden, it is natural that the potting shed should have a Christmas wreath.

Robbed of its foliage by winter, the twinkling lights entwined in the akebia vine become more prominent at nightfall and create a graceful and elegant frame around the door.

Having just a few friends over for drinks keeps the entertaining easy. The red damask cloth transforms an everyday table into a focal point making the season come alive with very little effort.

Invitingly Simple

For an uncluttered look, replace existing art with a wreath. It is an easy way to decorate, makes a strong statement, and fills the room with the fragrance of Christmas.

In Southern Mississippi, winter arrives very late. The fig vine on this pigeonaire is as green as a summer's day. Regardless, the structure is cleaned and decorated for Christmas for the pigeons to roost in style.

Naturally Fresh
Nothing says Christmas as loud and clear as all the fresh materials so plentiful this time of year. Fresh trees and garlands of cedar, spruce and pine, holly berries, nandina berries, and pyracantha provide us with a plethora of materials to work with. Gathering these items and putting them together can sometimes require more time, but usually very little energy is required in obtaining them. Purchasing fresh fruits such as kumquats, apples, oranges, persimmons, and pomegranates bring an old-fashioned and homey feel to most anything they are teamed with. Replacing the fruit as you indulge in it keeps the decorations fresh and you worry free from having it perish.

Decorating the Unexpected

When decorating, think of the areas you see or spend the most time in. These are usually the kitchen, family room, powder room or dressing area, as well as the entrance you use to access your home. Brighten up these areas with either arrangements, wreaths, bowls of ornaments or fruit, and you will soon be immersed in the spirit of Christmas.

❝ *Decorate the areas of your home that you and your family will receive the most enjoyment from.* **❞**

A tole container filled with Lady apples makes a pleasant and appealing holiday display. Today, Lady apples are used primarily for decorative purposes but also make a nice two-bite snack. Lady apples, originally cultivated by the Romans, are the oldest variety of apples known. The French considered them to be royal apples, and in the American colonies they symbolized wealth.

Votive cups randomly hung along this pathway light the entrance.

66 *Nature provides some of the most splendid creations for our enjoyment.* 99

An immense staghorn fern hangs from a tree along the driveway to Cedars Plantation.

Holiday Elegance

Tying It All Together

The decorations throughout this space show the importance of a cohesive design. The table top tree, newel posts, and wreath are all minimally decorated, yet give a feeling of opulence by the materials used. The gold silk embroidered ribbon on the wreath and the berry garlands tucked into the lush evergreen garlands, not only complement the room's colors, but are colors also used in the stunning arrangement (*opposite top*) of fruit, flowers, berries, and evergreens.

An exceptional set of sterling plates and goblets that have
been in the family for over five generations are saved and
used only for special occasions and at Christmas.

Using accessories that are the colours of the season transforms them into a holiday treasure that you might not have thought of previously using.

This beautiful Stuben vase takes on an even more holiday feel with the addition of Cunningham fir, ilex, tulips, and roses.

Traditional Style

Nothing intimates tradition and elegance more than silver, especially pieces that have been passed down through the family. Beautiful pieces of silver stand on their own, requiring no embellishment. *(above)* Ornate candelabra that normally hold ivory candles are now ready for the holiday by simply being changed to red. *(top right)* Pepperberry, tucked into an arrangement of green apples and paperwhites, blends beautifully with the shade of red on the walls. *(right)* A small bouquet of paperwhites makes a fragrant nosegay in this sugar bowl.

Looking at the reflection in this mirror, the decorations across the room, and in the opposite living room, appear blurred and dreamlike; only the cedar and berries in the forefront can be clearly identified.

A tea caddy filled with roses sits atop a Victorian beadwork stand.

Calming Beauty

As much as the expression "seeing red" embodies a feeling of strong emotions, blue sends a message of tranquility and peace. The strong red-orange walls and bold arrangement of roses and berries speak to us with a festive Christmas spirit. Once seated, the softness of the light blue china set against the sterling chargers brings a sense of serenity. Any anxiousness from the season's celebrations can easily dissolve.

(below)
The slight sparkle from the aged blue and silver glass ornaments is faintly visible in the arrangement of white roses, fir, and pittosporum.

From extensive travels, treasures picked up from all over the world work as fascinating decorative pieces throughout this home. Designing around a collection of ethnic art requires a very light-handed Christmas touch so as not to compete with the collection. A basket from Africa holds an arrangement of ilex branches that have been stuck directly into the soil of the staghorn fern, while a collection of South American malachite figures provides just the right touch of Christmas green.

" *Collections from travels unite to celebrate the season.* **"**

Changing the gold garland to red roses in this bowl shows how easily a different look can be achieved. With the advent of cold weather, the Chinese-style bird cage is moved indoors and used as a decorative accessory until warm weather returns.

An eighteenth-century European currier box used
by priests is a beautiful accessory and provides a
back drop to the St. Nick ornaments.

Balance and Beauty
Travel is the inspiration behind the creative collection of monuments displayed
on this table. Clusters of boxwood and pine separate the monuments giving the
appearance that each stands alone in nature. The pillar candles emit a glow in
the evening hours that provide uplighting to the large arrangement of holly and
ilex branches.

*D*elightful . . .

Candy Cane

Today the candy cane is red and white striped. It originally began as an all-white straight sugar stick, then in the mid seventeenth century at Germany's Cologne Cathedral, sugar sticks in the shape of a shepherd's staff were given to children to keep them occupied and quiet during the living creche productions. In 1900, the red stripes and peppermint flavor were added.

A mixture of home-baked goods along with candies purchased from the market make an easy and festive dessert party.

Tea Time

Cups and saucers are not just for restaurant use. They are beautiful pieces of china that lend elegance and sophistication to the drinks served in them. Tea in the afternoon only requires a few light bites, tea, and of course, an opportunity to show off beautiful accessories and fine linen napkins.

Afternoon Tea

Please join me for tea
Wednesday, December 14
4:00

~ Michele

This vintage ornament with blue trees is the perfect choice with
the bedroom's blue walls.

House guests visiting for the holidays
deserve to have their quarters decorated
just as the more public areas of the home.
A lush-mixed wreath and a single branch
of ilex and pine inside a vase make a
lasting impression.

> # "Remembrance, like a candle…
> burns brightest at Christmas Time."
>
> —CHARLES DICKENS

Decorative crowns from an extensive collection make symbolic and beautiful accessories on this table.

◄ The candelabra impart a regal quality to the winter dinner that awaits the guests. An arrangement of roses and pieris is topped with a pair of pheasants that complement the china and the woodland look of the table setting. Gifts surround the table-top tree on the English trolley.

◄ The cockscomb wreath and Burford holly arrangement take center stage at this intimate dinner.

A collection of North Carolina and Georgia pottery face jugs are ready for the holidays.

Dried hydrangeas make a beautiful wreath and add texture and dimension as a backdrop to the arrangement of cockscomb and pepperberries. Persimmons, while not long lasting, are a beautiful shade of orange that complement the softer shades of the hydrangeas and pepperberries.

Oranges and reds complement
each other here to produce a
rich and pleasing palette on this
oriental rug covering the end table.

(top left)
Santa goes fishing in a handmade dory purchased on Nantucket Island. The 1940's fishing pole, complete with fish on the line, belonged to a childhood friend.

(above)
A gold and black tole candelabrum not only adds ambiance to the room, but also helps bring the focus on the beautiful arrangement of accessories and flowers beneath it.

(bottom left)
Christmas is the ideal time to display this collection of small English bibles.

Before state souvenir spoons became metal with enameled emblems, collecting silver spoons was all the vogue. The spoons in this sweet collection have designs indigenous to each state's crop or flower it is known for.

▲ Serving hot chocolate should be more than opening a packet and adding water. Having a couple of friends over for homemade hot chocolate and muffins is an easy way to entertain. Using beautiful silver and fine china is also fun and festive.

An old fashioned cedar decorated with ornaments acquired over the years, and then strung with gold beads, is finished off with tinsel that is thrown on as opposed to being methodically placed on the branches.

Pretty Packages

Antique buttons make beautiful embellishments on gift wrapped packages. *(left)* Ribbon run through the buttons' back loop is fast and effortless for such an elegant presentation. *(right)* Vintage flower buttons are attached to the ribbon with a pearl headed pin.

A silver bon bon dish holds small ornaments of all shapes and sizes.

The knotted napkin not only adds interest to this table setting, but is also a clever idea if table space becomes an issue.

The use of cypress and the silver foliage of eleagnus adds contrast against the dark doors behind this arrangement. Southern smilax and the dense use of a variety of different holly berries and pyracantha make this composition a show stopper.

The sconce arrangements flanking the mantel are coordinated with the tree atop the piano *(right)*; however, additional holly has been added to the sconces for more volume.

A baby grand calls for a grand arrangement. Brown is a neutral color that when paired with green conveys a feeling of warmth. The tree is trimmed with magnolia leaves and chartreuse reindeer moss which add an element of softness and warmth while the red-orange ornaments and berries help to brighten the tree against the rich brown walls.

Sprucing it Up

Having an appreciation and collections of beautiful and fine accessories in your home provides many opportunities to easily decorate for the holidays. All decorative items seen on these two pages are objects that remain out year-round exactly as they are seen. By using fruit and blooming plants, kalanchoes in this case, and adding materials from the yard, each container provides a home for nature's bounty. Because some of the collections are large, a packed use of fresh materials in several of the containers adds mass and helps to unite the overall design.

A tea table in front of the fireplace makes an inviting spot for a celebratory occasion. The use of white with red accents is carried throughout the setting. The antique Battenburg lace mantel cover is accented with red candles and red holly berries; the white roses are also mixed with holly berries, and the scrumptious looking cake is topped with red raspberries. The neatly wrapped gift decorated with an antique rhinestone button, tops off this beautifully coordinated effort.

Set the Mood with Soft Lighting

(left)
Light from the single amber votive makes this an inviting spot for a cup of coffee.

(bottom left)
Angels fabricated from stiffened layers of gauze appear to be more lifelike with the shadows and glow cast by the candlelight.

(below)
Breakfast is served. The additional lighting from the lamp not only softens the morning ambiance, but draws attention to the Christmas decorations.

AMBIANCE

The mood one feels when entering a room will remain throughout the duration of the time spent in it. Lighting is one of the most important items for creating a warm and welcoming atmosphere. If the lighting is done well, then the addition of candles not only softens everything around it, but adds to the festivity of the Christmas season.

A basket of evergreens is a good solution for a door with windows since many times a wreath will hang too low. Additionally, the arrangement can be watered to stay fresh throughout the season.

General Displays

A beautiful late eighteenth-century hutch with its original interior paint houses a fabulous hand-painted collection of late seventeenth century commemorative china. Commissioned by Napoleon for one of his generals, these pieces were purchased in Paris and have since been passed down through the generations of one family. The simplicity of these small boxwood wreaths is all that is needed to further enhance the beauty of this collection.

(right)
Taking its share of the corner, this chubby little tree actually fills the space nicely giving the tree more presence in the room. The tree's natural woodsy look is retained with the collar of dried hydrangeas used at the base.

(below)
Beautiful appointments such as this Empire chest and exquisite mirror require very few trimmings during the holidays. Keeping a simple and low arrangement on the chest enhances the overall effect as opposed to detracting or competing with these lovely pieces.

(bottom right)
Standing guard over a bowl of pinecones and apples, these wooden figures purchased in India are a symbol of welcome. Traditionally placed at the front door, they make a welcoming statement on this coffee table.

> ❝ *First study the area or piece to be used to determine the scope of decorations needed.* ❞

The Magic of the Season

“Never worry about the size of your Christmas tree.
In the eyes of children, they are all thirty feet tall.”

—LARRY WILDE

"Merry Christmas to all and to all a Good Night."